Macaroni and Cheese Manifesto

Macaroni and Cheese Manifesto

BY

STEVEN H. BIONDOLILLO

First edition published 2009
Second edition published 2013

Third Edition

ISBN-10: 1977937624
ISBN-13: 9781977937629
Library of Congress Control Number: 2008906733

Visit www.amazon.com to order additional copies.

Cover Art: The Wrestler © 1993 Nancy Ostrovsky
Photography: Nancy Carbonaro

for those going the distance

CONTENTS

INTRODUCTION

Imagine beginning life the offspring of outlaws. Your Brooklyn-born father – Sicilian package of intense looks, edgy laughter and lethal hands. Your Manhattan-bred mother – sassy and utterly self-absorbed starlet, black sheep of an overachieving Jewish family, already-twice-married maneater.

The two meet ringside at the Copacabana and spawn three children – you're the out-of-wedlock first. Early life is 1950s unwholesome – an alcohol- and smoke-filled cup of nightclubs and late nights, racetracks and arenas, wiseguys and "relatives," day trips to Myrtle Avenue and the Rockaways, weekend trips to Stormville.

Imagine your father dies soon after your sixth birthday. His family cuts off your backbiting and demanding mother, your mother cuts off her smug and demanding clan. You and your siblings are on the way from the frying pan into the fire, as your mother willfully precipitates a freefall into a life of poverty and welfare.

This is you – always disheveled, usually hungry, often humiliated, regularly managed by maternal suicide threats. You're in and out of the hospital for everything from scarlet fever to head injuries to mysterious stomach ailments. You're not as good as others, you feel, except that you're obviously an exceptional athlete. Others seem confident and always to be talking. You just listen.

From a cigarette-burned kitchen table in an unkempt one-bedroom apartment in Queens, your mother rages against the world. She attempts to manipulate everything and everyone with whom she comes into contact, building up and tearing down in a vicious cycle of narcissism and destruction. Three years into the freefall a large private orphanage – a school for boys in Philadelphia – becomes known to her. This is her chance and, she presciently believes, yours.

Imagine now that you're a ward of the courts and on your way to that orphanage – the institution that will raise you for the next seven years, until you enter college. The social worker managing your case labels you "oversensitive" and "surly." The only positive thing in your life, according to the official report, is a tree-lined concrete playground a half-block from the six-story apartment building in which you live. Not even 10 years old, you are an unpromising cocktail of fear, anxiety and pride.

Now fast-forward 40 years. You're a business leader – an entrepreneur whose professional service firm is managing projects that employ over 3,000 people in 30 states. You're a pioneer in human services marketing and special-event fundraising for nonprofits. Events and marketing programs developed by you have helped worthy organizations acquire millions of caring donors and raise over $1 billion. You have achieved a measure of fortune and professional recognition. Your children live in circumstances that place them amongst the privileged.

How did this happen to you? How did you both survive the whirlpool and span the yawning socio-economic divide? How does one do it?

Simply put, one does not do it. In a word, it is not done by *one*. One needs others and, it turns out, many others. It is rare to have the opportunity – the good fortune in life – to be the priority of a competent adult. Legions of us have never had that opportunity – parent-child, master-pupil, mentor-mentee – a relationship in which for some meaningful period of time we were the priority of a reliable and focused adult.

Yet most of us at some point have had the opportunity to connect in one or more circles – teammates, classmates, co-workers, corps. If you've been lucky enough, you've been part of a circle which has confronted and survived great tribulation, strived to accomplish difficult and worthy objectives, experienced the pain and rewards of undertaking a campaign fraught with risk. Whether the arena is school, sports, work, service or war, you count the individuals from these circles as brothers. You might count the circles themselves, to paraphrase the Great Bard, as "bands of brothers." From these you have received most of life's difficult lessons and worthwhile fruits.

Like many, I owe both survival and success to experiences as part of several "bands of brothers" – my schoolmates at the orphanage, the fraternity of amateur wrestlers who strive in man's most grueling sport, the scores of my fellow business leaders committed to investing in our nation's communities, and the ancient brotherhood of bards – music- and meaning-makers whose songs cut through life's din, stretching and filling the chambers of our hearts and minds.

Contrary to a couple of our most enduring myths, one rarely goes the distance alone, or on the back of a single individual. The distance is traveled, more often, in a "band," which I like to imagine not as a blended group, but as a wristband with wide-set gems – each solitary, unique and valuable – tethered by common experience. This image, it seems, captures some of the essence of our paradoxically isolated and connected realities.

So, how, then, does one survive the whirlpool? By grabbing hold of that greatest of all life preservers – the solid ring of brotherhood. As the Reverend King might have noted, a foothold on the "rock solid foundation of brotherhood" might be the greatest of all blessings, as the ability to connect with *one* forms the basis to connect with *all*.

Just prior to my 10th birthday I was admitted to the nation's oldest large-scale orphanage, whose founder and ongoing principal benefactor is Stephen Girard (1750–1831), the great French-American businessman and father of American philanthropy. Girard, himself functionally orphaned by the age of 12, understood deeply that he was fathered not by a single individual, but by the thousands of human interactions that constitute life itself. Childless, he also understood that his own deeds and actions would in turn father others. "My deeds must be my life," Girard wrote. "When I am dead my actions must speak for me." Of all the great early-American patriots and freemasons, Girard meant business about brotherhood. I feel fortunate to be part of his hardheaded legacy.

Traveling a long distance in a short amount of time, whether practically or spiritually, can be a dizzying experience that leaves one grasping for touchstones. Sixteen years ago I set out to connect with others going the distance. I thought I'd draft essays; instead I crafted poems. For a professional public speaker and inveterate craftsman of the exceedingly dense essay, the metamorphosis into bard has been a natural one. The truth is, poetry is the only medium capable of containing in just a few "breath strokes" life's most disturbing dualities, irreconcilable differences and profound paradoxes. Hence, it is the only medium through which I have been able to get at some of my own improbable experience.

The title poem of this collection was selected for its obvious value: *Macaroni and Cheese Manifesto* – personal revolution, metaphor for those going the distance, poetry that sticks to the ribs. Please read with your mouth open!

(2009, 2013)

ABOUT THE POEMS

The poems collected in this volume were made to stop you, to stun you, even. They were surely made to be read – to be seen – and also to be memorized and performed – experienced out loud and in the flesh. They were made to be accessible and engaging, whether or not you know anything about my work or me, whether or not you know anything about poetry, literature or art. In two words, each of these poems is made to "stand alone."

In the introduction to her volume of essays, *Break, Blow, Burn*, literary and social critic Camille Paglia decries the demise of the "powerful, distinctive, self-contained" poem – the poem able to "stand up to all the great poems that precede it." In a similar vein, poet-critic Mary Karr, in her Pushcart Prize-winning essay on poetry, "Against Decoration," rails against the "highbrow doily-making that passes for art today," insisting that a poem meet at least two criteria: clarity and emotional impact. In his essay on baseball, "Opening Day, as Usual," the late poet-professor Jack LaZebnik might be sounding his own manifesto on poetry when he writes, "without suffering, there is no conflict; without conflict, no drama; without drama, no meaning."

Power, distinctiveness and self-containment; clarity and emotion; suffering, conflict, drama and meaning – shades of struggle, strains of salvation – spirit and beat in the blood of the street – this is what I offer you.

The poems collected here have been shared over the years in dozens of performance venues – meetings, conferences, class-rooms, workshops, banquets, retreats – not primarily with po-ets and academics, but with the broadest imaginable spectrum of laymen. Their narrative content ranges from the magic of city playgrounds and realities of elite athletics to heartbreaking current events and transcendent ancient and biblical conflicts. Each performance begins with the recitation of William Carlos Williams' gripping declaration – "It is difficult to get the news from poems, yet men die miserably every day for lack of what is found there" – which sets the stage for an audience-centered session of tears, shared insight, laughter and communion.

What I have the privilege of proving regularly, to paraphrase the title and upshot of poet-critic Dana Gioia's landmark essay,[1] is that poetry does, indeed, matter. So much so that I offer you, dear friend, a warranty: if you cannot find a single verse here that meaningfully moves you, please contact me. If money-back offers apply to virtually all manner of made things, why not to poems? One of them took me two years to make. All of them were made to move you. As you might expect, I am anxious to know if none does.

(2009, 2013)

---

[1] Dana Gioia, "Can Poetry Matter?" *Atlantic Monthly*, August 1991.

A new order shall arise and they shall be the priests of man,
and every man shall be his own priest.

—WALT WHITMAN

If beauty comes
it comes startled, hiding scars,
out of what barely can be endured.

—STEPHEN DUNN

{Strains of Salvation}

In Centerfield

It happened on a summer day
In 1965,
Our softball season underway,
The schoolyard was alive.

I'd shagged fly balls in centerfield
At least a thousand times;
The label on my glove had peeled—
Like me, its age was nine.

My dad had given me the glove
The day that I was born;
The gift outlived his hopeful love,
By six, my dad was gone.

A boy without a father seeks
A glade where he can grow—
A place where nothing hurts or bleeds,
A place where he feels whole.

For me that place was open sky
On ground of black tar seal;
While others tried in left and right,
I thrived in centerfield.

And so it came to pass that day
My solace was revealed:
With ease I'd made my umpteenth play,
While others lurched and reeled.

It melted through the sun's bright rays,
I heard it soft and clear—
His voice—I heard it plain as day—
His voice caressed my ears:

"My gift, my gift," the voice intoned
Right through the schoolyard din—
My graceful body is my home,
My home is deep within—

The revelation kissed my face
And soothed my wounds inside,
It told me how I'd find my place,
It blessed my fragile life.

A boy without a father seeks
A glade where he can grow—
A place where nothing hurts or bleeds,
A place where he feels whole.

I've lost my way a dozen times
And tossed away some years,
Been tagged out by my foolish pride
And gagged on my own jeers.

I want to hear the voice again,
To feel at home, to yield;
Yes, purge vainglory and false pain
To be . . . in centerfield.

(2001)

The Man in the Alley

In the time when our summers seemed endless,
And through streets and back alleys we roamed,
Then a game we did play
Off and on through our days
That belied that we all felt alone.

Yes the game was a break from roughhousing,
From bravado from sticks and from stones,
Was an urchin's main cope—
A high desperate hope
That in someone we might find a home.

Now this game was not played without danger,
It demanded one sneer and be wry,
Because no one could know
And no weakness could show
The prayer still behind steel curtain eyes.

Though the game was no more than a question
(But a question much more like a plea),
Its response might reveal
And its power might steal
Who it was that we wanted to be.

Automatically out burst the lit'ny,
The initial conservative list
Of distinctions and types—
Of predictable stripes—
The ones easy and rarely e're missed:

Someone strong, someone smart, someone crafty,
Someone fast and courageous and lean,
Someone brave and real quick
(With a chain! With a stick!)
Like a linesman, a pug, a Marine!

Someone bold, someone tough, someone nasty,
Someone hard and determined and mean,
Someone good with his fists
(With a blade! With a brick!)
Like a fighter, a wrestler, a fiend!

Marciano, Dick Butkus and Atlas,
Sammartino, George Patton, Joe Greene,
Mickey Mantle and Thorpe,
Flash and Thunderous Thor,
Man of Steel, Man of Labors, Bruce Lee!

So we boys cast about for our heroes,
For our fathers, our brothers, our friends,
For the question was *this*—
As we learned how to fish
For the answers to dictate our ends—

"If you found yourself caught in an alley
In a moment of ultimate need,
And a savior could choose
Or your life you might lose,
Then, pray, who would the perfect man be?"

No the church of the street is not pretty,
Yes it raises its sons o'er the knee:
"You shall reap what you've bought,
You'll become what you've thought,
Yea, the man in the alley is thee!"

So I speak with you plainly my brother,
For I've paid inconceivable fee,
When you're frightened and blind,
When your life's on the line,
Then the man in the alley is me.

Yes, the man in the alley is me.

(1998)

In Midtown

By St. Patrick's I asked for an answer—
For some sign that would help heal my heart,
In which sadness had spread like a cancer—
Why do some men survive a bleak start?

I had made my way up from the Bowery,
A lone pilgrim climbed clear out of hell,
I had sweated the street on that journey,
But now floated along with the swells.

There she sat on the steps of St. Thomas,
With her back to the rush-hour stream,
The great city flowed by decked in promise,
But she stared, as if lost in a dream,

At her compact, held close to her features—
Concentration, absorption and pique—
In her shopping cart life's comfort creatures,
In her hand some dark rouge for her cheek.

A teal sweater topped off all her layers
And black work boots proclaimed her large feet,
So collected was she, as in prayer,
Not a sweat bead betrayed the great heat.

For a moment or two the scene stunned me,
She looked focused and centered and strong,
That's why pity did not overcome me,
In a curious way she belonged.

57th and 5th brought the meaning—
Understanding of what I had seen—
The deep sense of impervious dreaming—
Understanding of where I had been:

Our proud mothers lived much like the homeless,
Yes like bag ladies, backs to life's stream,
All their powers spent shaping our focus,
Their cheap makeup made up our esteem.

They survived on received wisps of justice—
The sure scraps of the church and the state—
They rejected all those who might shun us,
Thus protected our delicate faith.

So, yes, sadness makes up my foundation,
Lo, the blush of success can't heal hearts,
No, in Midtown there is no salvation,
Fragile faith guides my steps toward the Park.

(2000)

A quiet conspiracy

A quiet conspiracy runs in the streets
    of a neighborhood in New York City—
Behind-the-scenes actors who manage to beat
    the "cheap sentiment" (what they call "pity"):

The butcher is in with his knife and his grin
    and the barber makes good with his razor,
The druggist contributes his pain medicine
    and the priest pitches in as a payer.

Yes each of them sees that young children in need
    want to feel and be treated like others;
I know this to be (know it personally)
    and can count for you some of their covers:

The butcher might say "free bologna today,"
    whispering *"ess und gedenk"* to his slices;
The barber might tease that "bald eagles fly free,
    cara mia!" then treat her to ices;

And when someone's sick, yes, the druggist might fix
    a small package to bring home to "mother";
And fees for their sports? Please don't give it a thought—
    Father Conlan has all the kids covered.

(Now, lo and behold, most young street kids can't know
    this design, through which they might grow faithful;
Can't grasp the faint tinkling of hope's fledgling notes,
    Yet must hope and have faith and be grateful.)

Thus actors, you see, and their actions indeed
   help to piece life together for urchins—
True charity's beat in the blood of the street—
   How "conspiracy" obviates doctrine.

for FEB and RCB

(2002)

A Single Word Emerges

"I'm not afraid to beat you up in front of your mother!"

With those words we were forever snipped from our mother's apron strings.

It was the first hour of our first day at the large orphanage that we learned, eventually, to call "Hum"—"the Hum," to be precise, as in not quite "a home," but a life-preserving refuge from our mother's dirty and degraded den.

It was orientation day for newbies and we were careening under the giant round table, swatting at the hems of the dozen or so flimsy skirts voluntarily surrendering their charges.

I'm not afraid to beat you up in front of your mother? The powerful, gravelly voice had stopped us cold. We crawled out hesitantly, flinchingly, to face it—Mr. Wileman was a giant bolt of dark suit, all thick twitching shoulders and "go on and dare me" black eyes.

Thus my younger brother and I were rescued from the chaos of our fatherless world and welcomed into the squirearchy.

I was just 10 and entering the 5th grade. Think: up till now, you've never brushed your teeth, eaten even one square meal or arrived anywhere on time . . . and today you're in the Marine Corps.

I have registered many of the Hum's usual first-year memories:

The seemingly endless recitation and singing of unfamiliar and discomfiting prayers, bible verses, graces and hymns . . . and the enforced silences of meals, work squads, study halls and bedtime;

The sting and confusion of a sly rap—the hollering human ring and frantic effort to stem welling eyes and strike back . . . and the shock and excitement of witnessing a wrestling meet for the first time;

The overwhelming size and openness of the physical plant— open-stall lavatories and shower chambers, 30-bed dorm rooms, four-acre playgrounds and museum-size buildings . . . and the totally inscrutable eyes and expressions of hundreds upon hundreds of boys.

* * *

Yet one memory stands out as a key to our collective life and future:

Every day at 3:15 Mrs. Knapp would signal to clear our desks. For the next 40 minutes she read to us, first from Saint George and the Dragon, then, later in the year, from the Legends of King Arthur.

Her soothing voice swept over the classroom like a sustained gentle rain on a desert. I, for one, had never been read to, and it seemed almost too good to be true that she read to us daily, and about the perilous times of bold knights errant and dangerous and deadly dragons.

Thirty years passed before I fully grasped—in one crushing, humbling moment—the genius and the generosity of Mrs. Knapp's reading of those particular stories to a group of wounded boys.

Yet, as I search my memory for a line from those many absorbing hours, only a single word emerges.

You see, at year's end our class performed a play for the elementary school, based on our readings, which followed King Arthur's trajectory from his days as a sweaty-but-hopeful squire to the point at which he addresses, for the first time, the fully assembled Knights of the Round Table.

As fortune would have it, the part of Arthur—and the lion's share of lines—had fallen to me.

And while I recollect Merlin gravely pronouncing, and the fun of on-stage swordplay, and the incomprehensibility of one classmate playing Guinevere and another the worm-like Lancelot, I can remember only this one word:

I remember it because it was a showcase for my "soon-to-be-teased-away" New York accent;

I remember it because it was a tough word for a 10-year-old to recite without eliciting snickers;

I remember it because it seemed to sum up the play;

And I remember it—still hear it these many years later—because it has carried and delivered the magical ring of meaning, and the feeling, the finality of a full stop.

"Brotherhood."

for Mr. Joseph Wileman and Mrs. Charlotte Knapp, with gratitude

(2001)

For the Athletes Unsung

Here's a song about playing the game—
    about glory and heartbreak and truth,
About three unsung men whose good names should be raised
    for the sake of the "red, white and blue."
They say "Winner take all!" is a natural call,
    but in truth it's a shame,
For a nation obsessed with one slice of the best
    chokes its children with pain.

Yes, these three once performed side-by-side
    with the best of the best in the land,
But because of some "twist" a great chance each did miss
    to alight on the stand;
Pray, what "twist" could engender a miss
    but the imperceptible truth—
A split second, a hair, an opinion, a stare . . .
    an odd phase of the moon.

So our story begins in Lake Placid,
    and ends with this now-famous line—
"Do you believe in miracles? Yes!"—
    and we all went along for the ride:
Thus the Stars-and-the-Stripes beat the Soviets,
    and ice hockey captured the gold—
Faith in youth, revolution and victory—
    a century's whole story all told.

In the haze of our wild exultation,
    things died that we all failed to see,
For Dave Delich, Jack Hughes and Ralph Cox,
    their young names and young hopes and young dreams;

You see these were the last of the players
    whom circumstance cut from the squad,
And I bet all the tea in old China
    that each felt abandoned by God.

While the victory band sailed in heaven,
    the souls of some men swirled in hell;
Oh those feelings, those feelings, those feelings—
    to many are known all too well:
Desperation and loss might describe them,
    or blackness or madness or pain—
Oh those feelings of rage and injustice—
    all prices of playing the game.

Now it's true about every dream realized
    that sacrifice has to be made,
But it's true that all winners with clear eyes
    do know where their debts should be paid:
While the usual thanks go to coaches,
    to parents, officials and friends,
It's the athletes unsung who prop high
    all who've won in the bittersweet end.

So remember the likes of Dave Delich,
    of athletes Jack Hughes and Ralph Cox,
They're your teammates in truth
    and your literal boost to that cereal box;
Sing a song for the likes of these athletes—
    a prayer for the athletes unsung,
For in God's perfect view—the simplest Truth—
    glory and heartbreak are won!

(2000)

[Note: The poet, a 1977 graduate of Boston University, was a competitor
in the 1980 Canadian Olympic Team Trials in freestyle wrestling.]

With hope and heartbeat

The wrestlers spring onto the mat,
Into the circle—human cats
Stunned and naked, bodies spare,
Relaxed and tense, inhuman stares;
Their breathing seething, set to pounce
As names and classes are announced.
Into this moment all contracts,
As primal need strains towards contact.

Their labors, dreams and wills imbue
This simple space, this time of truth,
With meaning and transcendent power—
The testing ground, the "crowded hour"—
Eternal struggle to control
One's life, one's destiny, one's soul.
Now here they stand, exploded view
Of human spirit, human roots.

Upon a time in Greece and Rome
Once wrestling champions were enthroned,
Assumed their places next to kings,
Inspiring throngs of men to sing
A body song, a dancing chant
Of rhythm, beauty, stealth and stance.
All those who sought the place of Jove
Embraced the way of blood and bones.

On this hard mat, in this cold hall
Young lions wait the zebra's call;
Though fear is near, desire's strong,
And to themselves they'll soon belong;
One simple thing would make them whole—
A single moment of control.
In history each seeks a home,
With hope and heartbeat, like a poem.

(2000)

The Distance

When taking
M E A S U R E
    of
      the
         MAN,
Mark both
    where
        he's
           L A N D E D
              and
        where
        he
BEGAN!

(2000)

The Bridge

I begin where the past ends and end where the future begins:
My dead were incapable of imagining me;
My beneficiaries incapable of imagining without me.

I am pure improbability,
An amazing alloy of unpromising elements—
Broken glass and sulfur, tinseltrash and sand.

I soar skywards from the swirling rush,
Stretch outward from the barren rock,
A self-made synapse, a sacrificial span.

I am will made manifest,
A mountain-shaped erection—
A dizzying achievement, an unnerving insurrection.

Fathered by my brothers, terrifying in success,
I have taken my impressive place
And taken your reluctant breath.

* * *

I end where the future begins and begin where the past ends:
My beneficiaries take me for granted;
My dead overtake me.

I strain towards a future I can imagine but not reach,
Reach for dreams I am not part of,
Promise lands I will not see.

I am a beacon and a touchstone, a compass and a cross,
My users are my living breath,
My future and my loss.

I sway before the ocean
And bow beneath the stars,
An isolated drama, my plea the only part.

Measured by my service,
My present is your path,
"Remember me 'til thousands thee . . . " my will and epitaph.

(1999)

The Captain

Glory.

Will;
Control.
Battle-hard,
Eye beams of steel,
Presence expanding.
Thunderous and shouting:
See! Chase! Clash! Strip! Kill! Clear!
Mine! Yours! Ours! All! Now!
The ground, the smell,
Sweat and gleam.
Serving;
Love.

Glory.

for RLB

(2005)

Corporal Tillman
1976–2004

Nourished by heaven's waters, tilled by firm hands,
He germinated in the rich, sun-drenched soil of boyhood—
    That level field upon which children and
    Their gods run and play—

Then grew, like most, in the hothouse—
    The potted pantheon of a nation's school system—
Before blossoming a strong specimen on artificial turf,
Where the masses gather weekly to worship.

Yet, possessed of a dogged intelligence, rare humility
And the deep sense of boyhood dreams,
He transplanted himself, re-centered, to foreign soil,
Upon whose rocky, storm-fed plain he was killed before taking root.

Today, we plant him again,
Now in the green and white garden of history—
    That rich soil out of which the past and future grow—
Where eternal yield provides a growing nation nourishment.

Let's give thanks for the wondrous conditions,
For the Planter and many magicians,
Who watered his dreams
And Spartan regimes.

(2004)

Because you feed me first

(The Hunter's Prayer)

"Because you feed me first," she said,
"Is how I know you love me."
(A central truth of life all told)—
My six-year-old shared bluntly.

TO THE SACRIFICED

I kill with a prayer of thanksgiving,
  And cook with a prayer for your part,
I serve to sustain all my living,
  And eat to fuel body and heart.

My heart is the key to my body,
  My heart is the key to my soul,
Your death yields the food that sustains me,
  My life is your legacy told.

TO THE GATHERED

We take that we might go on living,
  And give that we might never die,
Our days and our deaths are thanksgivings,
  We blaze and we die to give life.

We sacrifice self for our loved ones,
    And know that, in truth, food is love,
We're children, you see, of His Goodness,
    We eat now, while He waits above.

for SJK

(2012)

Poetry:

I've
Seen things
You people wouldn't believe:
Attack ships on fire
    off the shoulder of Orion,
I watched C-beams glitter in the dark
    near the Tannhauser Gate—
All
Those
Moments
Will be lost
In time,
Like
Tears
In
Rain.
Time
to die.

Poetry:
What's left,
Sometimes,
After loss.

(2007)

[Note: In italics—Roy Batty "Death Speech." *Blade Runner*. Dir. Ridley Scott. Warner Bros. 1982.]

```
        S
        U
        R
        R
L O V E
        N
        D E A T H
        E
        R
```

(after Louise Glück)

(2006)

Bright Light From Broken Places

"Bright light from broken places,"
    said the Angel of the Lord.
"He giveth and he taketh
    All, by mystery and sword.

In time most lives will fracture,
    Understanding might ensue;
For others life will shatter,
    Many cracks reveal the truth.

A single break yields insight's
    Light—a meaningful reward;
Myriad cracks create bright
    Light: Cold Fusion of the Lord."

* * *

Reb says you're never given
    Any more than you can take;
But Hell's now here, not Heaven,
    Hell says, "You He did forsake."

You're innocent—you're certain
    That your pain outweighs the crime;
And justice? Clearly broken;
    To your hardship He seems blind.

You yearn for daylight's healing,
     O, need badly some relief;
But daylight's not revealing,
     Daylight shrouds reality.

Plain truth shines through the night's sky—
     All creation on display—
No blinding sun to hide life's
     Facts—some billion suns, black space.

                    * * *

Dear friend, I know your anguish,
     Have been driven to my knees,
And studied Job's travails, which
     Do not seem to speak to me.

We're told to understand this—
     Told in this we must believe—
That pain in flesh and spirit
     Births our full humanity.

And so for now we struggle
     On towards some unclear reward;
Confusion…hope—all muddled
     As we seek to know the Lord.

(2009)

When I know...

... that the end of my days is near,
    Directly I will make a chair:

One leg will be made of the knowledge
    That billions have passed before,
Innumerable leaves in life's forests
    Succeeding *l'dor va-dor*;

A second will turn on the memory
    Of those who've given their lives—
The dutiful young who have died that
    Our land and our way might thrive;

My time here on earth, I'll remember,
    Is God's gift—not something earned;
That each of our days is a blessing's
    The feeling that primes the third;

The last leg will stand for my loved ones,
    In whose memories I hope to live...
"They can't see or know, yet will miss me"—
    Life's bittersweet take and give.

The seat and the back will be bracing,
    They'll show who's inspired me most:
The kings and the warrior-poets—
    Like everyman, come to dust.

The project completed, I'll gather
    My children upon the seat
To share with them two words of wisdom—
    Two words their young souls can keep:

While able, be sure to keep moving,
    Be never seated nor still!
Along the way pray for God's blessings,
    While working to know His will!

(2015)

[Note: *l'dor va-dor*—Hebrew for "from generation to generation."]

The Mountain

(My nigh destination)

So sorry it is taking me so long
(I think I see clearly,
I hope I am strong) . . .

Over the years I've made many a climb
That turned into a hill
or a dangerous mine,

Which accounts for my pace—often erratic—
Hot in pursuit, then
Coolly phlegmatic.

Yet the truest truth: I've settled for less—
Succumbed to some fear,
Camped out on a ledge,

Ducked into a cave,
Staked out a safe spot,
Irresponsibly played—justified lots.

But I sense, at last, the difference between
A worthy climb and
The other side's green.

Your summit's in view, I'm just about there,
Prepared to ascend
In rarefied air.

But what will I feel? Will I be worthy?
Not sure . . . that's the truth of
This matter and journey:

Breathtaking view? Some priceless perspective?
Worthy achievement?
Nearness to heaven?

A sense of belonging? Humble and kind?
Happy and peaceful?
And, possibly, tired?

Like much else in life it comes down to faith—
Yes, time to risk all—
No time to play safe.

I do want to reach you . . . rise up above . . .
Authentically know
The gift of your love.

For the mountain I climb—my end and my start—
My nigh destination—
Your beautiful heart.

for NFS

(2016)

30th Street Station

... cornucopia of things carried!

Cradled infant, child on shoulder, supported senior,
Luggage and bag, case and carrier, pocket book and pack;

Things carried, transported on silver steeds—
Palmetto and Pennsylvanian, Cardinal and Carolinian, Crescent and Keystone;

The porticoes are carried, too, by colossal Corinthian columns—
Sentinels at the entrance to this Temple of Transportation.

* * *

Here, Karl Bitter's reflexive masterpiece—his riot of restiveness—
Surges along the waiting area's west wall in bas-relief—

Spirit of Transportation—unruly parade of plow pulled by oxen, rider on horseback, and
Adiona herself—goddess of safe return—reclining, rere regardant on sedia gestatoria.

Then, in stunning reversal, a locomotive and ship carried forward in the hands of
Small children, led by an infant cradling a futuristic flying machine:

Labor, luxury, and imaginative leap crowned by wheel-and-wing,
Uniting earth and sky, toil and spirit.

* * *

Yet the pièce-de-résistance soars solemnly at Center Station:

A lifeless body—slain soldier from the Pennsylvania Railroad's ranks—
One of 1,300 who laid down their lives—

Clutched from the flames of war and carried heavenward in the sure and mighty hands of
Michael—Angel of the Resurrection—terrible transcendent transportation—

Handiwork of Walker Hancock—earthbound sculptor, spirit transporter, maker extraordinaire.

* * *

Adiona, Christopher, Lord protect us.

And when our journey's over, O Michael,
May we be as worthy as your naked charge;

Carry our broken bodies back, we pray,

... in your hands!

(2016)

{Shades of Struggle}

Macaroni and Cheese Manifesto

We are what we eat, it's been said.

Well, as long as I can remember, I've been eating macaroni and cheese.

One of my earliest food memories is the big, bright-orange block of cheese sitting next to the gunk pot on the splattered stove in our apartment's yellowing speck-of-a-kitchen.

Big, bright-orange, purple-stamped block of government surplus, it was—ever-present prop whose shavings fed the ever-present pot.

Occasional visitors could hardly conceal the "what the hell is that!" expressions on their faces.

In those days only welfare recipients *made* macaroni and cheese. Everyone else just stirred up the processed kind.

The Great Society provided sustenance in shocking dimensions—was the intention to feed or shame us?

We usually felt ashamed.

Nevertheless, we hunkered protectively over our sweat-seasoned bowls eating, as we were scolded, "like there was no tomorrow."

* * *

Other early food memories revolve around occasional outings to Horn & Hardart—never-since-surpassed nexus of industrial and culinary efficiency—gleaming steel counters and clattering trays, shining tile floors and revolving beehive food dispensers.

We always got the macaroni and cheese, which had a baked, golden-brown crust that we couldn't get at home.

And because each of us had his own dish from the beginning, and because you had to pay before you could eat, we ate there, usually, without much anxiety.

* * *

Yet the high point of our experience with macaroni and cheese was that rare trip to Pippo's—there we would quickly gobble three or four baskets of bread and butter, then linger over orders of baked ziti and ravioli.

The owner knew us.

These were the only meals of childhood that I remember eating slowly.

* * *

Wandering through my kitchen today one hardly notices either the speckled cheese roundlets sitting on the marble platter near the microwave, or the small library of cookbooks on the counter adjacent to the gas range.

Perusing a title recently I was reminded of a recipe that I had seen en route to the West Coast, in one of those in-flight magazines offered between hors d'oeuvres and entrée.

A recipe for macaroni and cheese.

"What the hell is this?" I remember thinking—macaroni and cheese evolved from staple to gourmet preparation.

The revelation had jarred then subdued me, like news of the demise of a childhood friend.

I stand in my kitchen today the remainder of an improbable journey up the food chain.

We are what we eat, it's been said.

But it's also been said, and so it would seem, that the cheese stands alone.

The cheese stands alone.

(2000)

13th and Arch

I still see them circling—
Unholy mix of killers and
Carrion creatures—
Staring, leering, sniffing, calling.

I look up into their faces and
Reach for the sleeve of my
Nine-year-old brother's suit jacket,
Pulling him close.

It's drizzly, and the bottoms of my
New black leather shoes are
Slipping on the
Scummy pavement.

I raise an arm towards the approaching
Stream of swishing wipers—
Thin black fingers wagging
No, no, no, no.

The taxis here are a strange mix—
Not the yellow cabs with the
Helpful lights
I'm used to.

Some slow down to
Look us over,
A couple circle the block to have
Another look.

We're due back at the
School, where the front gate
Guard will give the
Driver a voucher.

Our two-hour bus ride had
Turned into three; my confidence that
We'll make it is
Slipping.

I pull my Irish twin closer and
Step towards the
Pay phone:
"Watch them."

0-212-ST4-2709
The rotary is sticky:

"Operator."

"I'd like to make a
Collect call from Steve."

"Surely."

One ring. Two rings. Three rings. Four rings.
My ears begin to burn.

"Hello?"

"This is the operator.
Will you accept a collect call from
Anyone by the name of
Dave?"

"Steve!" I practically shout.

"Yes."

"Mom?"

"Stevie."

"Mom, we're in Philadelphia at the
Bus station. We can't get a cab.
I can't get anyone to
Stop."

* * *

As I'd done many times,
I held my breath while
She assembled
The truth:

"And what would like me to do about it?
I'm in New York."

* * *

It was a long time ago, and I have
No recollection of how those
Two boys in little suits survived that
Stygian eve. No recollection whatsoever.

But my mother's retort—the
Sting and bite of the naked truth—
That sticks with me still:

"And what would you like me to do about it?
I'm in New York."

(2013)

The *lekh l'kha* imperative

The *lekh l'kha* imperative sounds forth from deep within—
The truth—not many hear the call, its pitch above the din:

Confront your weakness, do what hurts, at all cost make things right,
Grab failure by its bloodstained shirt; engage, it's time to fight!

The still, small voice of self-disgust says, time to sacrifice;
The still, small voice says, truth or bust—redeem your fractured life!

Like Jacob you've usurped a place; the truth—you're in the cold;
The truth—yours *is* a nameless face; it's time, reverse your hold!

The naked truth is only grasped by those of us who hear;
Hence, *sh'ma's* the point all things repass; yes, then do things adhere.

Our lives are won in mortal strife—our chance to measure God;
It's we who force day out of night . . . *sh'ma* . . . *lekh l'kha!*

(2003)

The Boy He Could Not Save

I saw a strong man pause to cry
And asked what caused him pain.
He drew a breath and this replied,
"The boy I could not save."

I knew this man, he never lied,
He never spoke in vain.
It came then as a great surprise:
A boy he could not save?

His character was true and wise,
His record bore no blame.
I hoped he would identify
This boy he could not save.

I gently probed, he blinked and sighed
But would not give him name.
"Just look into my eyes,"
He said, and then he strode away.

I'd looked into his steadfast eyes,
Reflected on his fame.
I saw a strong man forged in fire
Who deftly bore life's pains.

For many months I sought this prize:
To know the boy he claimed,
To know the secret of his eyes,
To know his sigh and pain.

Who was this poor boy who had died?
This victim of life's flames—
It was, of course, the child inside—
'Twas *him* he could not save.

You see, a strong steel's forged in fire,
For man it's just the same.
The price of strength is sacrifice—
The child cannot be saved.

(2001)

Thanksgiving Receipt

Her first Thanksgiving back from college my daughter sprang out of the Town Car and started up our front walk. We circled her en route: hugs and kisses, some explanation of a not-so-faded Division I ding, and an afterthought—"Here." She handed me the large, easy-to-read receipt—bright yellow testament to distance traveled—$58 from the airport.

I turned to start back up the walk reminded of a freshman year over two decades earlier, when $50 represented a social security payment—total monthly living allowance—the paltry receipt of a father's choice not to pay into the system.

A surge of gratitude for blessings present melted into the mixed memory of Thanksgivings past: the motley gathering circling the tin folding table, turkey parts and Del Monte cans orbiting the steaming bowl of instant stuffing; and the drawn and self-contained high-school boy layered in hooded sweatshirts and neck towel, mid-section carefully wrapped in plastic begged from dry cleaners, curtly rejecting entreaties to eat—"I'm sucking weight."

Out of the cramped apartment, on the empty streets of Thanksgiving night, the ritual would begin: jog to the corner, cross the deserted avenue, stretch and roll on the cold, hard safety mats beneath the playground's swings, then begin pounding towards the bowels of Long Island City—industrial Queens.

At the 39th Street drop in Skillman Avenue, Midtown's glittering skyline would suddenly expand—the cue to narrow focus to next week's season-opening meet. I'd begin the internal drone—"Who's the champ? Who's the champ? I am. I am." Past the giant factories and their empty truck bays, under els and over train bridges, along the perimeters of refuse-strewn lots, monotonously, interminably chanting, pounding, paying the price, praying the price.

Seeing my teenage daughter bound effortlessly, happily into our home her first Thanksgiving back from college playing fields, it occurred to me that I have no memory of returning from those long-ago, inner-gritty Thanksgiving runs—no homecoming memory in hand, but, thankfully, a bright receipt for a price paid.

(2001)

Materfamilias

Ours was a two-acre sliver of asphalt clinging to a precipice overlooking the unrelenting
     landscape of industrial Queens,
A concrete oasis pushed to the brink by blocks of six-story apartment buildings,
A world of bars and blacktop and chainlink backdropped by the majestic Manhattan
     skyline,
A haven on the edge of a New York City sardine-can neighborhood with the unlikely
     name of Sunnyside.

Torsney playground! Breughelian masterpiece of old gossips stuck on park benches
     and busty young mothers with baby carriages,
Of screaming little bodies on see-saws and swings, and shuffleboard sticks
     with their stick-figure old men,
Of hardheaded beauties behind diamond-fence backstops and their legions
     of skirmishing teenage gladiators,
Of working-class men in their compact kingdom, all bottle-bags and bravado.

Desperately we streaked to you from our holes and our hells and learned everything
     in your hard embrace:
That everyone is part of the picturesque pot and even the fat kid gets picked,
That beauty and badness are kissing cousins, and fisticuffs and forgiveness
     functional friends,
That we all bleed alone in sundrenched corners while the glorious scene swirls on.

Now gratefully we tumble back to you and count the blessings of our youth:

To have been fathered by experience and had experience father-forth our fathers,

To have fallen for our first loves—round and rubbery, taped and laced, frizzy-haired
    and freckle-faced,

To have forever the capacity both to feel and be free, bred on your soft and
    stone bosom,

                                  at your indifferent knee.

(1998)

King of Concrete

I'm the King of Concrete,
    Yo, I sing of the street:
Cruise my sidewalks, cross the gutters,
    Get in step with my beat!

I'm the King of Concrete—
    No Boy Blue, no Bo Peep:
Turn my corners, count the streetlights,
    Be alert and be fleet!

I'm the King of Concrete,
    Hear me bring on the heat:
O the backfires and the sirens—
    They're my chirp and my cheep!

I'm the King of Concrete,
    You can't fathom my feet:
Spy my scrapers, check the sewers—
    They're so high and so deep!

I'm the King of Concrete,
    The thick crowds are my peeps:
Feel the closeness, bump the bodies,
    Join the crawl and the creep!

I'm the King of Concrete,
    Smell the rank, taste the sweet:
Skirt the curb crud, what's yo flava?
    You can hide here or seek!

I'm the King of Concrete,
    I laugh loud and I shriek:
On my playgrounds, in the alleys,
    You can look or go leap!

I'm the King of Concrete,
    Have some havoc to wreak:
Screw your time up, twist your mind up,
    Make you cuss—bleep, bleep, bleep!

I'm the King of Concrete,
    I can make grown men weep:
Crack your ego, shake your soul, yo,
    Cause your body to bleed!

I'm the King of Concrete,
    It's respect that I seek:
Know the tragic, feel the magic,
    Still yourself, take a knee!

(2011)

Consumatum Est?

Yes, *Consumatum Est*—
I witnessed it, did you?
His face, his eyes—they said it—
My time has come, adieu!

Like all true kings he seized it—
The final moment—truth;
A true king must conceive it—
His time of death—his proof.

He staged the final moment
For all the world to see,
A radical atonement—
This man of thirty-three.

His heart—Siberian darkness,
His will—a conquering tool,
The hill he chose—Olympus,
For thirteen years he ruled.

Like those who ruled before him
He yearned to swallow space,
To own life's vast condition,
To dominate the race.

He chose as his successor
Another shaped by plains—
By endless sky and weather—
Pure-driven as the rain.

Not since the time of Arthur
Has brotherhood reigned strong,
Save in the minds of grapplers
Do kingdoms carry on.

Some say it was a forced slip,
An accident, lost time;
To me it looked deliberate,
It looked to me divine.

His face, his eyes—they said it—
My time has come, adieu!
Yes, *Consumatum Est*—
I witnessed it, did you?

for Aleksandr Karelin and Rulon Gardner

(2000)

Because I was poor

Because I was poor
My life began with naught,
With fear and shame;

Because I was poor
I prayed to God for truth,
For life and strength;

Because I was poor
I bought the path—
The longest, hardest way;

Because I was poor
I paid full price—
Red blood, white tears, black pain;

Because I was poor
I stayed the course,
Surviving fire and rain;

Because I was poor
I earned it all—
My skill, my soul, my place;

Because I was poor
Now I am rich,
With money, friends and fame;

Because I was poor
My inside bleeds,
My outside reads disdain.

for Andy Hug, 1964–2000

(2001)

The other shoe

The other shoe—

Visiting the iniquities
Of the fathers upon the children
Unto the third and fourth generation of them that hate me—

I'm waiting for it to drop.

Are you?

(2002)

Memo to Job

Memo to Job:

Faith in the Lord
Is its own reward.

Who knew?

(2002)

Rough Beast Born

In the beginning were the haves and have-nots,
And they dwelled together in the wasteland.
And you said, let there be television. And there was television,
Shining your cold light even into the have-nots' caves and crevices.

For many seasons the have-nots shivered in your shadows
And stooped beside the stream of your cold blood,
Unable to quench their thirst,
Bowed by images of what they could not have or become.

The snow spirals:
And now I see how your banality is overcome by the revelation of our reality—
How your images of our lives capture your women who take our essence,
And our issue captures your world with our strength, which takes your essence.

Thus, logically, the new order has come to be,
The new world has come to be.
Rough beast born,
Baby.

(1999)

480 B.C.

"Suddenly the piled mass of the dead gave way. An avalanche of bodies began. In the Narrows the allies scrambled rearward toward safety atop a landslide of corpses. . . . So grotesque was this sight that the Hellenic warriors . . . discontinued the press of their advance, looking on in awe as the {Persians} perished in numbers uncountable, swallowed and effaced beneath this grisly avalanche of flesh."

from *Gates of Fire*
Steven Pressfield

About salvation, he is on the money, Pressfield—
He shows in *Gates of Fire* how freedom itself—
The fragile beginning of Western democracy—
Is saved—in 480 B.C.—
By a band of Spartan warriors.

In a feat of Maccabean magnitude,
300 men—each purposefully selected
By the Spartan King Leonidas
To stand and die
At the narrow pass of Thermopylae—
Hold off an enemy
Nearly two million strong
For a period of seven days,

During which time
The inchoate Hellenic alliance
Rallies enough
To begin turning back
The ambitious Eastern tide.

                                   ***

When asked, what thought should win one's mind
When at the brink of death,
The tried Dienekes this replied
In words that struck direct:

"Not daughter, son nor loyal wife
Can conquer mortal fear;
Save brother by your side who fights
Can galvanize your spear.

"The opposite of fear is love
For brother put to test;
His heart's what you have knowledge of,
His life makes rich your death."

*

Great Leonidas this apprised
When asked, how did you choose
The men you did to stand and die—
The men you chose to lose:

"When the world looks to our nation
For strength in face of doom,
Who will offer *us* salvation?
Dear mothers, it be you!

"Defying pain, with clear dry eyes,
You'll sing our heroes' praise;
Within the story nothing dies—
Your love, their deeds, our way!"

*

At last Xeones lets us see
The source of freemen's drive;
An orphan, slave and wounded, he
By choice does stand and die:

"A man will strive to be the best
He possibly can be,
If in his heart he knows his quest's
A meritocracy."

Thus men of action live and die
And, clear, describe their cause:
"Go tell the brethren here we lie,
Obedient to their laws."

for the firefighters, police, emergency medical personnel and armed forces who, in AD 2001, stood and died

(2002)

[Note: *Gates of Fire*, Doubleday, is the title of a novel by Steven Pressfield. Dienekes, Leonidas and Xeones are three of the novel's protagonists. The phrases "stand and die" and "the opposite of fear is love" are from Pressfield's text.]

Odyssean Encounter

Cocksure
      I plunged
            into
                  your dangerous waters.

I had been
      chopping through
            your shallows
                  for quite some time—

Easily eluding
      your erratic breaks,
            contemptuously kicking
                  your foamy dribble—

Insensate
      ruler
            of
                  my knee-high kingdom;

Almost instantly
      I recognized that
            your power
                  was practically absolute;

My senses
      screamed
            on
                  your salty roller coaster,

My body—
      like a cork—
            was unsinkable
                  yet helpless—

In control of
      its new destiny,
            in control of
                  nothing;

I surrendered
      to
            your great sucking
                  force,

Riding
      your rip
            along the
                  shore,

Buoyed
      by a desperate
            interior
                  patter;

Then,
      a mile away,
            you suddenly,
                  unexpectedly

Disgorged, slamming
      my body
            onto the
                  broken-shell beach,

Shoving me away
        through the shard
                and pebble
                        and sand.

Now
        cut and burned,
                dazed and denied
                        I make my way

Back along the beach,
        tearfully
                back towards
                        my unclear kingdom,

Disillusioned
        and bowed,
                empty and
                        uncertain.

(1999)

Dunblane

From the unfathomable depths of the northern sky
    charges Michael, gallant and grim,
Reaper of the righteous, terrible swift arm of the
    Almighty;
Evil has struck within,
Heaven strikes back:
A victory for Darkness in a trove of small children.

The errant Archangel, conveyor of warriors,
    gathers the fallen precious in,
Where they will glint eternally, golden bits on his
    Mighty Shield;
Glisks in the universe
Blinding God's eye:
Everlasting reminders of glorious life, and death.

(1996)

{Tributes}

A version of this article originally appeared in The Wall Street Journal.

The Father of American Philanthropy

"My deeds must be my life." This was the exceedingly simple credo of the now practically forgotten father of American philanthropy – Frenchman and Philadelphian Stephen Girard.

A down-on-his-luck sea captain, Girard arrived in America in 1776 at age 26. Taciturn and hardworking, he pursued vastly successful careers as a mariner, merchant and banker, becoming over the years the new nation's wealthiest citizen.

Above and beyond his business affairs, Girard built hospitals and risked his life and fortune bailing the city of Philadelphia out of the yellow fever epidemic of 1793. With John Jacob Astor, Girard personally financed the War of 1812 for the U.S. government.

To the childless Girard, however, these accomplishments weren't enough. "When I am dead, my actions must speak for me." With these stark words, Stephen Girard bequeathed his entire estate, some $7 million, to create and sustain a school – a "college," as he called it – for orphan boys. At the time of his death in 1831, Girard's estate was the nation's largest. In the 182 years since, his gift has proved to be the most generous and prescient contribution to human service in the history of the U.S.

This decidedly unsentimental businessman, who could have built any number of grand and glorious monuments to himself – libraries, museums, parks – instead dedicated his wealth to providing comprehensive practical support (food, clothing, shelter and education) to a bunch of fatherless boys.

Let's put this in historical perspective. During the final years of Girard's life, Horace Mann was still years away from realizing his dream of public education. No state provided free primary school education; secondary school opportunity existed only in church schools and in the academies that prepared the sons of the wealthy for college. Girard's decision to provide free education for *poor* children was, for all practical purposes, a revolutionary clarion call.

Since the opening of Girard College in 1848, more than 22,000 indigent boys (and, since 1984, a few hundred girls) have passed through its magnificent gates bound for college and other productive paths.

That is to say, more than 22,000 indigent kids have been rescued from the streets and raised as sons of Girard. Based on the most modest calculation, Girard's combined progeny since 1848 would equal in number the population of a major American city. Now imagine that city almost entirely full of an underclass. Throw in for good measure a handful of world-class criminals. The economic and social impact on the nation, the drain on its resources and threat to its institutions, would be staggering.

Girard's most important legacy, however, is not the social violence and economic desperation that he forestalled, but the thousands of productive lives that he made possible – my own included. I happen to be one of his sons. For seven years – from the fifth grade until I entered college – he fed, clothed, sheltered and educated me. He bought the milk and cereal, baked the casseroles and cookies, provided the soap and toothbrushes, furnished the sneakers and baseball gloves, darned the socks and sweaters, sent me to the barber and the doctor, provided the books and lab supplies and much more.

While millions of Americans have passed through the entrances to Carnegie's library, Guggenheim's museum and Rockefeller's park preserve, I promise you that precious few of them drop to their knees on a daily basis to give thanks to these grand gentlemen.

On the other hand, there are thousands in the U.S. who go to bed each night of their lives with praise on their lips and a prayer in their hearts for Stephen Girard. Imagine, thousands of individuals today who owe their opportunity for a good life to the vision of a man who has been dead more than a century and a half. Just think of how another half-dozen or so bequests like Girard's could alter the destiny of the nation.

A version of this article originally appeared in Amateur Wrestling News.

To a Giant

Here's one for the "little sprouts" of the sports pages. A tribute to the most "Muggsy Bogues-like" of all amateur sports. An apologia for the most marginalized major athletic activity in the United States. Wrestling.

After four decades of carrying on his shoulders a couple of worlds, one of wrestling's few living giants has stepped down. Most people are born, live and die without ever meeting a giant. In mythology the role of giants is to birth and support universes. Throughout human history they have founded our nations and their great institutions.

Like all giants, Coach James C. Peckham is larger than life in more than one world and in more than one way. His well-earned retirement has left Harvard University without a distinguished wrestling coach, Emerson College without its founding athletic director, the world of amateur wrestling in New England without its original bedrock, and the international wrestling community without one of its largest local landmarks.

Let's meet Jim Peckham, then, and discover why his is not a household name.

It has nothing to do with his athletic achievements. He was a member of the 1956 U.S. Olympic Wrestling Team, a National AAU Champion, and 15-time New England Champion.

STEVEN H. BIONDOLILLO 81

It certainly has nothing to do with his coaching credits. He has coached the Olympic Team, World Cup Team, Pan Am Team and New Zealand Games Team, some of them several times.

And it most definitely has nothing to do with his community-mindedness. For over 25 years, Jim Peckham was the heart and soul of the Young Men's Christian Union at Boylston and Tremont Streets, near Boston's Combat Zone. He was a permanent fixture in a day when blue collars and blue bloods pursued elite amateur athletics together in community-based gymnasiums, in the time before restrictive multi-million-dollar university facilities and tony health spas.

It was at the Union that Coach Peckham, a chiseled granite hulk of a man, met and took under wing a small black youth from Roxbury named Kenny Mallory. Coach Peckham coached – no, let's say raised – that youth to become New England's only native-born NCAA Wrestling Champion.

Imagine that! In one of the world's most internationally-renowned cities for poor race relations, an unprecedented and profound human victory played out without a single spectator. No newspapers, no parades, no public kudos.

No, the reason Coach Peckham is not a household name has nothing to do with his achievements. It has something to do, however, with the ethos of the man and his sport.

"Being a winner is not a right," reads the big sign in Harvard's wrestling room. "You must constantly earn the right to win."

Like life, and unlike most sports, wrestling is among those rare athletic endeavors in which the most vicious phases of competition do not happen on "game day." They happen daily, as the wrestlers struggle with their own changeable levels of desire, determination and discipline; and weekly, as they "suck down" body weight and "wrestle-off" with teammates in order to earn the privilege of competing for their teams. No, at the end of the day in wrestling, there is not one ounce of physical or psychic energy left for the press or the public relations pros.

And this, unfortunately, is the way many of the media's mavens would have it. Because wrestling, quite frankly, scares the hell out of them. Too many sports journalists, it is no secret, are former football- and basketball-player wannabees, comforted no doubt with the fact that they were not adequately endowed for the big time . . . you know, the genetic thing.

In wrestling, however, there is no excuse – genetic or otherwise – for not becoming a champion. The sport favors neither height nor weight nor body type. It's what I like to call the "Muggsy Bogues Dilemma." Here's a guy – 5'3" – making hay in the NBA. Why is no one covering him? Because Mr. Bogues reminds all of the former wannabees that, in terms of the big time, they just couldn't cut it . . . you know, the inability-to-perform thing.

Unlike most sports, wrestling presents to prospective participants one of life's rarest phenomenons – the truly level playing field. Accessible and affordable for all, wrestling could have a unique and important role to play in a nation being mugged by growing legions of disaffected youth.

Back to the mat.

Jim Peckham is not a household name because the media has shut out the nation's sixth-most-practiced sport at the high school and collegiate levels.

Nonetheless, it's a shame that no one covered Coach Peckham's retirement dinner. Old lions from every corner of the United States attended the standing-room-only function to pay tribute to the giant and his wife Jean. They recounted a few wrestling war stories, and remembered some of the hundreds of kids whose lives have been saved by the wrestling fraternity. Mostly, however, they spoke in a philosophical way about community, brotherhood and love.

A roomful of warrior-poets, I thought. Physically potent, philosophically profound.

The most moving tribute of the evening came in the giant's own words, but not directly from the giant. It turns out that, for many years, Coach Peckham has put out his own personal newsletter to a couple thousand individuals who have been part of his universe. Each newsletter contains three or four articles on subjects such as integrity, religion, racism, friendship, marriage and the like. As part of the tribute, one individual read a portion of one of the Coach's articles, at the conclusion of which there was not a dry eye or unhugged body in the house.

And I overheard one woman at my table saying to another, "They don't make 'em like this anymore, do they?" A fitting tribute to the Coach, I thought, but fundamentally untrue. I should have said to her, "Welcome to the world of wrestling – where no youth ever failed to grow in equal measures physically, mentally and spiritually."

So here's my tribute, Coach – a tribute undoubtedly in the hearts of all the old and young lions in the room. I'd like to take it back to childhood, to the most basic of schoolboy "hypotheticals," to the time of life when all schoolboys desperately search the landscape for men big enough to be father, coach and mentor all rolled into one.

"If I was in a dark alley, and had to go back-to-back with one person to save my life, and I could pick only one person in the whole wide world to go back-to-back with . . . "

Enjoy your retirement, Coach. Step down, but don't go away. We may need you.

A version of this article originally appeared in Amateur Wrestling News.

My First Wrestling Coach

My first wrestling coach, Robert Ayjian, recently passed away. He was 59 years old. His nickname was "Age," which is how the first syllable of his last name is pronounced. In the winter of 1967-68, Age both introduced a group of us sixth graders to wrestling and coached us during that critical first year. I say "critical" first year because, as we all know, if not introduced properly, a kid might drop out of any sport, let alone wrestling, which is much more demanding than most.

I hope that you might now be calculating Age's age during that winter of 1967-68. You have calculated correctly if you have deduced that, when I was in the sixth grade, Age was a high school senior. At the institution in Philadelphia in which we both grew up, elementary school students were introduced to wrestling by our high school's seniors, who we called "biggies." "Biggies" were bigger versions of us. Who were we? We were a collection of several hundred fatherless boys, all wards of the courts of Pennsylvania, being raised at Girard—the nation's oldest large-scale orphanage.

While it is common to be introduced to a sport and/or formally coached by a teenager, it is entirely uncommon to experience that in the context of an orphanage—a type of "peer society." Most children, at the end of a school day, go home to a parent or guardian who will inquire about the day—ask how the day went, provide encouragement, express pride. In a peer society, however, the experience of this type of individual attention and reinforcement is rare. After all, how likely is it that a teenage boy who has experienced scant individual reinforcement might learn to be supportive of his younger peers?

Which is why Age was so special. He was that rare teenager who could not only set goals and expectations, run an intense practice, and make things fun, but could also verbally articulate pride in his charges. That's right, Age could say, "I am proud of you." To many this may not seem like much. For legions who have never had the good fortune to be the priority of a focused adult, however, these words can be life-changing.

My high school, college and elite wrestling careers were rewarding enough. I won a handful of medals in national and international competition and had the privilege of serving as a coach, for five years, on the staff of a NCAA Division I varsity program. That said, I was not the best high school wrestler whose career Age can claim to have launched. That pride of place goes to my high school classmate and training partner, Danny, who won the national championships and finished his illustrious high school career with only a single regular-season defeat. Age was very proud of Danny.

But Age was also proud of me.

Every five years since 1973, I have returned to Philadelphia for our orphanage's high school reunion. Sure enough, Age would be there. He would grab me, tease me a little bit about his nickname for me—"Meatball" (which was not a slur, but an accurate description of what I looked like as a roly-poly 11-year-old in oversized sweats!), then escort me amongst his friends explicitly expressing pride in my long-ago wrestling accomplishments. This ritual—Age, a head-to-toe-tattooed Viet Nam veteran and motorcycle mechanic, bragging about me, a buttoned-down marketing executive—has always been the secret highlight of my quinquennial high-school reunions.

Now, all of a sudden, it will be no more. Which is why I write.

I did not have an opportunity to thank Age adequately for getting me started in what has to be the world's most challenging athletic enterprise. As we all know, no sport prepares one to rebound, press on and succeed in life better than wrestling. How lucky, then, was I? A ward of the courts who had the good fortune to grow up in an institution with a wrestling program breeding the likes of Robert Ayjian—capable, big-hearted and generous as the day is long.

Truthfully, I can count on a couple of hands the number of times in my life I have heard from a father-figure the words, "I am proud of you," which would not be inconsistent with the reality of many who grew up without fathers. And half of those times, I humbly account, were compliments of Robert Ayjian.

It is with a mixture of sadness, gratitude and, yes, pride, then, that I share with you this memory of a recently-passed-away member of our wrestling fraternity—Robert Ayjian, my first wrestling coach, of whom we might all be proud.

The Gift of Adversity

Midnight tonight will mark the 51st anniversary of my first step towards the world of wrestling, because at midnight tonight, exactly 51 years ago, my father passed away at the age of 46. I was just six years old and in the first grade.

It would be an understatement to say that my father was born into a set of challenging circumstances. He was the fifth of six surviving children of Sicilian immigrants living in hard-scrabble Brooklyn, New York. His own father was an intermittently-employed hard drinker with a mean streak.

In his early years, my father's principal assets were prodigious athleticism and a pair of highly-skilled and devastating hands, which enabled him to survive a childhood on the streets and a stint in reform school, where he was introduced to a breed of men ironically called "good fellas," whose ranks he would eventually join.

Among the dozen clear memories I have of my father are a handful that I cherish: in particular, learning to ride a bicycle, learning to hit a baseball, and, with my 11-month-younger brother, learning to box—a skill that had earned my father, in the circles in which he traveled, legendary status both on the streets and in the ring.

You might now be thinking those fraternal boxing matches were my first step towards the world of wrestling, but that would not be the case. After my father died, my mother's circumstances dwindled, and our family slipped into a life of poverty, welfare and crime. Then, three years after my father's death, when I was nine years old, my mother learned about a school for fatherless boys in Philadelphia called Girard College for Orphans, and arranged for my placement there.

Thus I became a ward of the courts of Pennsylvania and began my seven-year tenure in the nation's oldest large-scale orphanage, which rescued me from a chaotic life in New York City and provided me for the first time with stability—predictable nutrition, adequate clothing, medical care, a good education, and (the most important thing to this nine-year-old boy!) abundant athletic opportunity, including the sport we are here this evening to celebrate.

Entirely unbeknownst to me, I had arrived in the mid-Atlantic state generally recognized to be the cradle of wrestling in the eastern United States, and at a school of several hundred boys in which many (if not most) of the best athletes wrestled. I remember witnessing, as a 10-year-old fifth grader, my first wrestling meet. I had arrived in Pennsylvania from the New York City public schools, where wrestling was a TV spectacle and fighting strictly forbidden. Now here I was, watching—live-and-in-person under the official auspices of a school—two partially-clad boys tangled up in an all-out brawl. It was shocking, exciting, almost dizzying! I thought... was this going to be expected of me?! I play baseball for goodness' sake! I'm a shortstop and centerfielder! What's going on at this crazy school?!

A year later, as an 11-year-old sixth grader, I found myself dressed in oversized sweats and rolling around on a mat in Girard's subterranean wrestling room. Our elementary school team was coached by our varsity team's co-captains, who, to their endless credit, provided a wonderful introduction to what all of us here know is a very tricky enterprise to launch successfully.

Thus began my wrestling career, which would unfold in three separate eras: six years at the youth and high school levels, where I became a two-time Philadelphia-area private school champion and one-time runner up, as well as a place winner in the National Prep School Championships; five years at the college and elite levels, where I twice qualified for the Canadian Intercollegiate Athletic Union national championships and placed fourth in my second attempt, as well as had the opportunity on a half-dozen occasions to represent both Canada and the United States in international competition; and, finally, five years as an assistant coach in Boston College's Division I wrestling program.

Like all wrestlers of a certain age, I have dozens of wonderful stories to share, many of them true! But in the interest of time, I will share only a single story from the very beginning of my competitive career, as well as some of the important lessons learned from that experience, after which I will sum up my professional career, which, as Harvard's wrestlers might say, is what earned me a place on the podium this evening.

The story I will share is from my second year on the mat, when, because of my status as an undefeated 12-year-old eighth grader (I had skipped the seventh grade), I was asked at season's end to wrestle a varsity match. As far as I've been able to ascertain, it was the very first time my high school had tapped an eighth grader for a varsity match, let alone a 12-year-old eighth grader. I weighed 88 pounds, but was inserted into the varsity line-up at 103 to replace our injured 103-pounder. Our varsity's 95-pounder didn't bump up because he was protecting an undefeated season.

The experience of putting on (and swimming in!) the varsity singlet and tights, donning the varsity warm-up jacket, running through our ad hoc pep squad's 30-yard-long human tunnel to the mat, and circling the mat in front of a screaming home crowd was spine-tingling and surreal.

As most of us here know, I would be the second in our line-up to wrestle. To say that I was in a state of shock doesn't quite get at the state I was in. Without exaggeration, rigor mortis was setting in! In an attempt to bring me to, one of our school's baseball coaches climbed out of the stands, grabbed hold of my headgear and started shaking: "Can you hear me, Steve, can you hear me? Wake up! Come to, buddy!"

Well, the inevitable happened: I was hoisted onto the mat and landed, stunned, at the feet of... the Jolly Green Giant. My opponent was 16-years-old, almost two heads taller, and 15 pounds heavier. And, as if he wasn't large enough, he actually struck the Jolly Green Giant pose, hands on his hips, arms spread wide, looking bemusedly down his nose at... Little Sprout.

Let me quickly recount for you the ensuing blur: ready, wrestle; I shot; scored the takedown; hung on for the period; chose bottom; sat out; turned; caught the Giant's head... and pinned him! The explosion in that gymnasium was deafening. It was one of only two times in my entire competitive career that I jumped into the air in celebration of a victory.

While there are many truths and lessons in this story that have shaped both my athletic and professional lives, I will share only a handful:

First, many of life's opportunities and challenges present themselves suddenly, at which point you can choose either to climb into the arena or stay out of it. One of our greatest presidents, Teddy Roosevelt, famously said: "The credit belongs to the man in the arena." I say, always choose the arena.

Second, many (if not most) of life's worthwhile challenges are big and hairy and green—two heads taller than you are and 1,500 pounds heavier. The larger the risk in any enterprise, the larger the reward. Always choose large goals and objectives, worthy opponents, and worthy enterprises. Remember, you become what you think: therefore, think big!

Third, a little fear is a healthy thing, and useful. It has often been said that one thing all successful people have in common is fear of failure. Too much fear will paralyze you. Too little can lead to cockiness, or deprive you of the juice and the drive that most of us need to succeed.

Fourth, never underestimate your opponent. Looks are deceiving. Little Sprout is happy to take you down. Practically every military strategist in history has noted that underestimating one's opponent is the first flaw in a failed campaign. Always bring a healthy respect and your whole game to whatever challenge you face.

Lastly, never disrespect your opponent, either in victory or defeat. Right now you might be thinking that the Jolly Green Giant staring down his nose at Little Sprout was disrespectful. Perhaps. But the less disputable truth in that long-ago wrestling match is the more egregious expression of disrespect was Little Sprout's leap into the air. I should not have done that. I remember that, when I lost the bronze medal match in the National Prep School Championships to a wrestler hailing from one of the nation's other orphanages—the great Milton Hershey School—my opponent did not jump into the air. Instead, he took me by the arm and walked me to my corner, which was a very classy thing to do. Win or lose, always be classy.

I have taken these and many other lessons learned on the mat into my professional life and career. As many of you know, I founded the firm that gets the credit (or, depending upon your opinion about this type of fundraiser, the blame) for sparking the national renaissance in walkathons. We did not invent walkathons; we brought them to scale by organizing the world's first million-dollar walk, $2 million walk, $3 million walk, and so forth. In *USA Today*'s listing of the nation's "Top 10 Charitable Fundraising Events" are three walkathons designed and/or meaningfully developed by my firm. Those would be number one, number three, and number eight. Number eight alone involves over 700,000 participants and three million individual check writers, who collectively contribute in the fight against breast cancer over $75 million per year.

Along the way, our firm has become the nation's leading special-event fundraising educator, training over 13,000 nonprofit staff. The net result of our efforts has been to catalyze a $2 billion walkathon market, as well as elevate and professionalize the entire field of special-event fundraising.

Big numbers aside, let me tell you what our most important achievement has been: by developing the world of peer-to-peer fundraising—walkathons, bike-a-thons, and the like—we have given average American citizens, as well as citizens with extremely modest means, the opportunity to be philanthropists. Because in walkathons you ask your friends, family members, neighbors, and coworkers for small contributions to support the causes that are dear to you, the nation is now teeming with caring people of modest means who routinely raise tens of thousands of dollars. My team and I are proud to have helped unlock the potential of grassroots giving in the United States, and to have prefigured many of today's trends in political and online fundraising.

So where are we headed next? As we changed the world of special-event fundraising, our firm is now aiming to change the world of "corporate team building." What currently passes for "corporate team building" technique seems to be off-the-mark: one thinks of ropes courses, "escape the room" games, bicycle-building projects, theater improv, and scavenger hunts.

Thinking differently, our idea is… if you want your team members to have a deeper understanding of each other, and you want to put them in touch with their inspirations, as well as build their commitment to the team… they must face each other in a circle and (no, not wrestle!) talk. But not about anything. Specifically, they must talk about their "Gifts" (all the amazing things life has bestowed upon them), their "Thoughts and Inspirations" (all the individuals past and present who've captured their imaginations), and their "Actions" (the things they are actually doing that will, when they are dead, serve as their footprints). Gifts, Thoughts, Actions!—three words that can meaningfully describe and predict the arc of one's life.

While I would love to share with you my personal response to all three of these powerful words, I will end now by sharing only what I believe are life's three greatest gifts:

First and foremost is the *gift of life* itself. I say a prayer of thanksgiving to God, and to the father I never had a chance to know, who died 51 years ago this evening and never had another chance to give his sons a hug: thank you for life.

Second is the *gift of adversity*. Yes, adversity—the never-ending series of experiences, challenges, and forces which shape our lives and characters. Whether you're a two-year-old struggling with your laces, a child struggling with a musical instrument, or an adolescent struggling with peer pressure… whether you're a student struggling with algebra, a breadwinner struggling to make ends meet, or a business professional struggling to meet competitive challenges... whether you're a young boy struggling with the death of a father, a plunge into a life of poverty, or a seven-year stint in an orphanage, you should say a prayer for the life-shaping gift of adversity. We know from the biblical story of Jacob wrestling the Angel two things: that God will challenge us, and that wrestling—the metaphor for sport itself—is also the quintessential metaphor for the entire human experience.

And last, but not least, the third of life's great gifts is the *gift of community*. Some of us are lucky enough to be born into productive families and communities, while others of us choose and/or create them. Whichever, all of us, in meaningful measure, are defined, supported, schooled, inspired, propelled, and validated by the communities we are part of.

Which is why I am humbled to stand here before you. My wrestling career, my business career, my life are as much your achievement as mine. You, the people in this room, have defined me, supported me, schooled me, inspired me, propelled me and, now, validated me. The nation's renaissance in walkathons... the fact that Americans of modest means can now be philanthropists... the $2 billion peer-to-peer fundraising industry that supports so many worthwhile causes... these are, in meaningful measure, your achievements, too—the achievements of our collective wrestling community, which exists to protect and promote life's most perfect level playing field—the mat!—on which kids like me—who might never have had a chance—learn to survive, succeed, and flourish.

As I walk away from this platform, I thank you from the bottom of my heart, and ask all of you to give yourselves an ovation and, maybe, even a hug, but for goodness' sake no "body locks"!

ACKNOWLEDGEMENTS

The many staff at Stephen Girard's great school, who, when we were schoolboys, required us to commit verse to memory

Professor Helen Vendler, who, when we were undergraduates at Boston University, taught us how to read

The late Professor Donald Theall, who, when we were graduate students at McGill University, taught us, in his year-long seminar on *Finnegans Wake*, about making sense

Alan Jacobsen, my first sounding board for this project

Rod Buttry and the Boston College wrestling family—my first public audience

Sharon Shaw, whose thinking influenced the selection of title poem

Nancy Ostrovsky, whose art graces this volume's cover, and her partner Paul Widerman, the inventor of SmartBells

Nancy Sackheim, who improved my introduction

Daniel Young, whose intuitive grasp of this project has been unsurpassed

Alan Bergstein, Howard Brodie, Dave Collins, Chris Cox, James Curran, Rocco D'Alleva, Alan Jacobsen, Frank Killoran, King Lenoir, Jerry Myers, Benjamin Venafro, and Brad Wallin—the round table

The best ever of my executive assistants, Jean Kaiser, and

My children—Rachel, Anthony and David—whose innumerable contributions over the years have improved most of what is contained herein—

I thank you all.

ABOUT THE AUTHOR
Steven H. Biondolillo

Steven H. Biondolillo is the founder and president of Biondolillo Associates, Inc., a marketing and development consulting firm dedicated to helping nonprofit organizations build special-events and other creative fundraising programs. Biondolillo is widely recognized both for sparking the national renaissance in walkathons and for coining the term "signature event." Additionally, he has developed what is regarded to be the nation's premiere training program in the field of special-event fundraising. Since 1984 fundraisers developed by Biondolillo have raised over $1.2 billion.

Biondolillo has been a guest lecturer at the Wharton School at the University of Pennsylvania, the College of Communication at Boston University, the Carroll School of Management at Boston College, Emerson College, Babson College, the School of Continuing Studies at Georgetown University, the University of Massachusetts College of Management in Boston, the Kellogg-Recanati Graduate Arts Administration Program at Tel Aviv University, and the Executive Program for Nonprofit Leaders at Stanford University's Graduate School of Business. Additionally, he has appeared on several national network and cable news programs, including NBC's Today Show, Fox News, The O'Reilly Factor and NPR.

Until 1983 Biondolillo was an elite freestyle wrestler and medalist in national and international competition. He was a member of the coaching staff of Boston College's NCAA Division I wrestling program. His op-ed pieces on amateur sports and child welfare have appeared in publications throughout the United States, including *The Wall Street Journal*,

Chicago Tribune, Atlanta Journal-Constitution, Miami Herald, Philadelphia Inquirer, Boston Herald, Boston Globe, Boston Business Journal and *Union Leader*. In 2013 Biondolillo was inducted into the National Wrestling Hall of Fame as an Outstanding American from Massachusetts.

Biondolillo completed graduate work in English Literature at McGill University and language studies at the University of Grenoble. He received his BA in English Language & Literature from Boston University. He is also a graduate of the U.S. Army War College's National Security Seminar.

ABOUT THE ARTIST
Nancy Ostrovsky
by Barbara Pollack

Nancy Ostrovsky is a pioneer of performance painting, an art form that has not yet been embraced by galleries and museums, but has earned her a dedicated following. Just as jazz musicians often go unrecognized, Ostrovsky has forged her own path in art without worrying about who's hot and who's not. Instead, she has spent her life absorbing influences and processing experiences, then putting it all back into her paintings, which have grown more expressive and wise over the course of the past three decades. For more information: www.nancyostrovsky.com.

A curve ball . . .

Black-Blue & White!

Two tribes roam the streets of the City,
    Their colors like helmets and crests—
The Black-Blue & White of the Yankees,
    The Bright-Blue & Fire of the Mets.

"Black-Blue & White!"
    "Bright-Blue & Fire!
We'll sizzle you, Stripes, 'cause we're high tension wire!"

"Bright-Blue & Fire!"
    "Black-Blue & White!
We'll bust your big head, Metropolitan Blight!"

The number of calls one might think of
    Is limitless... try it, it's true;
Then next time you circle the other,
    Call out the bad beats made by you!

Our purpose, you see, is creative...
    We share a deep love of this game
Of curve balls... and poems which begin with
    Monsieur Valéry's "ligne donnée"!

(2016)

For information about Biondolillo's inspirational teambuilding and leadership development seminars, please visit www.biondolillo.com.

Visit www.amazon.com to order additional copies.

This book is set in Garamond type.
The cover is set in Typewriter.

Made in the USA
Columbia, SC
16 March 2018